Heritage Embroidery

Plate I   MERTON. Designed and embroidered by Elsa S. Williams.

Heritage
Embroidery

ELSA S. WILLIAMS

VAN NOSTRAND REINHOLD COMPANY
NEW YORK   CINCINNATI   TORONTO   LONDON   MELBOURNE

Acknowledgements

This book is dedicated to my competent and industrious staff who have worked with me during the past several years to produce fine embroidery materials for American needlecrafters. Their sincere cooperation is deeply appreciated.

I want to express my gratitude to my associates and students whose embroideries appear in this book, and to all the needlewomen who have joined me in promoting the art of embroidery. Their requests for designs and their enthusiasm has been the inspiration for much of my accomplishment. I am also grateful to my editor, Clara Fried Zwiebel, whose guidance in arranging my words has resulted in saying what I really mean.

I owe my heartfelt thanks to my husband, mother, and daughter who have lived with my needle and thread projects; traveled with me to faraway places to promote heritage embroidery, and have provided me with the encouragement and creative peace which has made possible the completion of this book.

Elsa S. Williams

Van Nostrand Reinhold Company Regional Offices:
New York Cincinnati Chicago Millbrae Dallas

Van Nostrand Reinhold Company International Offices:
London Toronto Melbourne

Copyright © 1967 by Litton Educational Publishing, Inc.

Library of Congress Catalog Card Number 67-24700

Printed by Maple Press
Bound by Maple Press
Designed by Anne Hertz
Drawings by the author
Photographs by George H. Boyer

Published by Van Nostrand Reinhold Company
450 West 33rd Street, New York, N.Y. 10001

Published simultaneously in Canada by
Van Nostrand Reinhold Limited

16 15 14 13 12 11 10 9 8 7 6 5 4

Contents

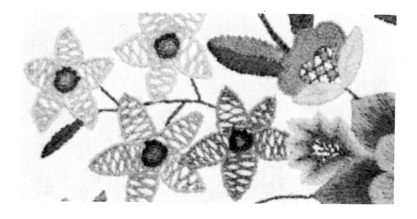

Foreword

Elsa Williams believes that she was first introduced to embroidery on the day that she was born. The first child of a missionary couple in the prairie lands of South Dakota, her first clothing was made by her parents, using the best material they had available. The designs were those her father adapted from a Sears Roebuck catalog and the embroidery was worked by her mother on linen that had been a wedding-gift tablecloth.

Her childhood was lovingly programmed by her maternal grandmother whose chief interest was "handwork." Therefore, it was not surprising that the author completed a cut-work banquet cloth and a dozen matching napkins by the time that she was twelve years old.

Later, attending art school, she discovered a talent for design which was further developed during her professional career as the art director for a publishing company. These accomplishments, a love of needlework, and her talent for design were two of the compelling factors which, in 1950, resulted in the establishment of her own company in West Townsend, Massachusetts, producing needlework materials which are sold all over the country for creating Heritage Embroidery. Her lifelong respect for fine needlework is reflected in the high standard of these supplies which include only the finest fabrics and thread to be worked into valuable heirloom pieces.

A constant search for authentic designs and the best materials for working them has taken her to meet gifted needleworkers, both cultivated and primitive, in many distant and obscure corners of the world. Her lecture tours in America are not only popular but reflect her deep satisfaction in pioneering the art and furthering the traditional interest in fine needlework in her own country.

Introduction

A renaissance of embroidery has developed in American needlework during the past few years and with it an appreciation for fine embroidery pieces of heritage value. Much credit is due to the interest promoted by our great national restorations where beautiful old embroideries are included in the famous collections. Surely those in Williamsburg, Virginia; Deerfield and Sturbridge, in Massachusetts; Winterthur, Delaware; and Shelburne, in Vermont have made us aware of the value of fine handwork. Through the medium of television thousands of American women have been inspired by Jacqueline Kennedy's successful efforts in authentically recreating the original rooms and furnishings of the White House. These and many smaller yet similarly purposeful projects have inspired many to participate in the art of hand embroidery for home decoration.

The success of this new interest in embroidery must, however, be attributed in large measure to the increase in women's knowledge. Advancement in education brings with it the ability to appreciate beauty and the desire to participate in worthwhile projects. Consequently, the intelligent modern woman is not interested in putting stitches over printed lines or producing a piece which is exactly like another. Creative embroidery provides her with an opportunity to think while doing. The use of beautiful colored threads combined with a variety of stitches becomes an exciting and stimulating challenge.

Because the modern renaissance of stitchery consists chiefly of crewel embroidery, this book will deal particularly with crewel. The instructions and technical advice may be applied to other forms of needlework but are presented here principally as they apply to crewel embroidery.

In recent years a number of excellent books have been published wherein the emphasis has been on certain rare and beautiful pieces located for the most part in museums and private homes inaccessible to the great majority of needlewomen. However, in the full realization that many fine embroiderers do not possess the skill necessary to develop designs worthy of their craftsmanship, but who, nevertheless, wish to participate in creating pieces of lasting value, this book aims to provide information and designs using materials which are readily available at most needlework shops. If, however, any difficulty is encountered by the reader in locally finding precisely what she seeks, she is cordially invited to communicate with Needlecraft House of West Townsend, Massachusetts.

Tree of Life design by Louise Chrimes. Embroidery by the author.

CHAPTER ONE

The joy of embroidery

The excitement of creative accomplishment is one of life's most satisfying experiences. By combining stitches with colors, the embroiderer discovers this joy when a design outline becomes a colorful work of art which reflects her personal taste. Like the painter or sculptor, the embroiderer is rewarded with the visual result of her efforts.

As soon as the novice discovers the joy of embroidery it results in an enthusiasm which touches the lives of others. I have known many beginners who eagerly shared their pleasure with others who, in turn, soon became involved with their own embroidery projects. One of the real dividends of this handiwork is the new friendships it creates. Not only in community project

groups and sewing classes, but also for the traveler. Wherever embroiderers meet, they share a common bond and an absorbing interest. A few years ago my daughter and I found overnight accommodations in an Austrian farmhouse. Before leaving for a neighboring *Gasthaus* to have our evening meal, I complimented the farmer's wife on her small handmade doily which lay beneath a vase of flowers on the hall table. When we returned we found that she had added two night tables at each side of our bed with *Guten Morgen* and *Gute Nacht* embroidered on the covers. A beautiful topsheet was on the bed with a wide border of hand crocheted edging and a beautiful pillow was embroidered with garlands of flowers entwined around the words *Nur ein viertel Stunde* (Only one quarter hour) indicating that it was to be used for comfort during a short mid-day nap. Although she could speak no English and my German was rather feeble, it presented no problem to us. Our communication was based on our admiration for each other's handwork.

More recently I had the opportunity to teach crewel embroidery to some native women of the Azores. In preparation for this activity we learned a few Portuguese words from a record but we found that we needed these words only for travel convenience. The women who were already expert embroiderers expressed their enthusiasm by showing me their work while my own embroideries and fingers imparted what skills I have, to them. It was a most rewarding experience. I recommend embroidery as a travel dividend to anyone who enjoys meeting the people of foreign lands. Language differences are no barrier to the embroiderer who can appreciate a beautiful needlepoint rug in a French château or an embroidered napkin in a peasant's home.

For most busy women, embroidery has become a hobby or avocation. In my grandmother's day this was called a pastime. It was a diversion from routine and perhaps a worthy form of recreation. Today we place more emphasis on the value of our time and, consequently, it is no longer a pastime but rather a time for avocation to produce something of distinct value. I am sure this is why so many embroiderers are concerned with heritage pieces for their homes and have discontinued making less important bits and pieces of expendable handwork.

From the standpoint of avocation, many embroiderers find much satisfaction in sharing their knowledge and skills where therapy is sorely needed in hospitals and nursing homes. I urge you to discover this great joy if you have not already done so. Some extraordinary embroidery has been done by men who eagerly learned to embroider while confined in Veterans' and private hospitals. You will find that hospitals and nursing homes are most appreciative of the services of volunteer workers who can inspire their patients and distract them from their ills. The patient who attempts embroidery in therapy often finds it a lifetime interest.

It is also important to remember that the joy of embroidery may be imparted to children. A part of our responsibility to continue the making of heritage needlework is to teach the art to children so it extends to future generations. If I ever have a granddaughter I will be certain to teach her as soon as she can manage a needle. Every stitch will be pure fun instead of an unpleasant drill as it was in my childhood. Big ones, little ones, fat ones, thin ones, lumpy ones, crooked ones, any kind of stitches at all. The joy is the important part; excellence comes later.

If you are already dedicated to the art of needlework, you are aware of the personal satisfaction one feels for having completed a lovely petal or a beautiful leaf. If you have experienced the pride of accomplishment, you have a deep appreciation of excellence when you see it in the intricate work of other dedicated artists. All these joys can be yours when you participate in the art of heritage embroidery producing heirlooms for the future.

This, and all other illustrations in this chapter, are stitch details of Merton, embroidered by the author.

Betchworth. Designed and embroidered by the author.

CHAPTER TWO

The value of Heritage Embroidery

We must, of course, express our gratitude to the Early Colonial needlewomen who brought with them, and executed in great quantity, their heritage from the Old World. The skills they learned in their native lands and the materials they were able to bring to the New World provided the beginning of what we now treasure as Early American embroidery. The value of many of these pieces cannot be estimated in dollars. The inspirational value is enormous and the heritage value is beyond measure. Fortunately, there are many pieces which have been preserved from that era, to be seen all over America.

Unfortunately, however, we cannot be proud of many further achievements in American needlework during the past century. We can, perhaps, attribute some of the blame to the machine age. The development of machine-made laces and embroideries has been remarkable but they can never qualify as works of art of any heritage value. During this period when machine-made pieces became available at low cost, it destroyed much of the incentive and desire for hand-done work and consequently, we find very few noteworthy museum pieces of needlework which were produced by the 19th-century embroiderer.

In recent years we have developed a better sense of values concerning handwork. We owe our gratitude to expert needlewomen, such as Louise Chrimes, who have kept the art of embroidery alive during the past decades. Their devotion to heritage embroidery has provided us with the inspiration to continue needlework which is deserving of preservation.

The practical application of embroidery usually determines its value for the modern woman. While a sampler has its purpose as a tool for learning stitches and techniques, it nevertheless has lost its appeal to most needlewomen. Also, the embroiderer who values her time and wishes to create a piece of real value can no longer be interested in embroidering things like pot-holders or pillowcases which are expendable. Instead, she prefers to create a piece which is individual and which she cannot purchase ready-made. It may be a sweater embroidered with a lovely rose to make it a distinctively original garment, or a handbag with a colorful design added to match her costume.

Candle Sconces. Designed and embroidered by the author.

The embroiderer who desires to create a piece which will surely become an heirloom finds great satisfaction in working something for household decoration. An embroidered picture can be the work of either a novice or an expert needleworker. There is no limit to the uses of embroidery for the home: pillows, mats, chair seats, curtains, bedspreads, rugs, lampshades, mirror frames, book jackets, luggage racks, etc., are only a few items. These pieces and many more such items will last for hundreds of years if good materials and good design are combined with carefully executed embroidery.

The choice of design contributes in large measure to the value of a piece of embroidery. A design which is poorly drawn does not have as much value when compared to one which is more carefully executed. When we examine the work of great artists we are constantly aware of their particular attention to pattern and form. This must also apply to the art of embroidery.

Of course every needlewoman is not capable of superb designing and many will need to work from kits and printed patterns. The prepared kit is useful for the beginner who is not able to work with a qualified teacher, but it is important to choose kits which permit the embroiderer to produce a finished piece which is not necessarily a duplicate of thousands like it. When the design limits the embroidery to solid masses of Satin stitches and Outline stitches it provides little opportunity for individual distinction. This is also true of stamped Cross stitches which merely require placing thread mechanically over the printed linen.

Strawberry tea cozy designed and embroidered by the author.

Whenever possible, I like to encourage needleworkers to create their own designs, for this is when the work has its greatest value if the execution is distinctive. When original designs are not dealt with successfully, it is perfectly possible to create an embroidery of exceptional value by working from an available masterpiece design. These patterns by outstanding designers and from museum collections are usually provided without diagrams or directions. This permits the embroiderer to select her own colors and make her own choice of stitches. The result will be a piece which is the only one like it in the world, for it is not possible to duplicate hand embroidery exactly when working with this method. It is then, in effect, an original embroidery.

Tree of Life tea cozy design by Louise Chrimes, embroidery by June Clark.

Personal pride in possessing such a piece of original embroidery cannot be measured in price. Nevertheless, it is important to realize that an embroidered application to a chair, for example, would indeed increase its monetary worth. Consider two identical antique chairs, one with the chair seat upholstered in fine fabric alone, and the other covered in beautiful crewel embroidery. The hand-embroidered chair is immediately considered more valuable and with the passage of time the embroidery has increased in heritage value, while the fabric-covered seat becomes worn and frayed and has less and less worth.

Although this appears to be an original Colonial piece this Paul Revere footstool embroidery was designed by the author in the style of 1776.

Plate II CHERRY TREE. Designed by the author and embroidered by Rebecca Wilkinson.

CHAPTER THREE

Crewel embroidery

The revival of interest in crewel embroidery during the past years has made us aware of the fact that this type of needlework is truly heritage embroidery. When we examine the museum collections of various types of embroideries it is interesting to discover that crewel work on linen fabric has had exceptional lasting qualities while most silks and cottons have become brittle or have deteriorated in color and form.

It is, therefore, important to know what constitutes real crewel. Genuine crewel threads are made of fine twisted wool from exceptionally long, strong fibres. It does not have the glossy, hairy quality of Persian yarns which are used in rug work. The long haired fibrils used in crewels are twisted many times in the process of making the thread and this produces the strength which accounts for its durability. For heritage embroidery I urge you to use only strong, 2-ply fine crewels which are available in beautiful colors. Since the fine fibrils imbue thoroughly it is possible to dye them all the various shades of a color from a very dark hue to the very lightest.

Crewel embroidery *must* be worked in crewel threads. Embroidery worked in any other thread does not qualify as crewel. Some commercial crewelwork is produced using only Chain stitches. This is usually hand-hooked from a bobbin, in continuous rows, and is not considered good crewel embroidery. A design worked in Cross stitch using crewel wool should not be called crewel embroidery; it should be classified as Cross stitch worked in crewels. When needleworkers refer to crewel embroidery, they are refer-ring to wool embroidery worked in a combination of several *different* stitches.

Embroidered by Grace O'Neil

Designs for chair seats adapted from floral forms of the Stuart period and embroidered by Rebecca Wilkinson and Grace O'Neil.

Embroidered by Rebecca Wilkinson

Embroidered by Grace O'Neil

Embroidered by Grace O'Neil

Outline, Long and Short, Chain, and French Knots are a few of the basic stitches. Therefore, a design worked in a combination of several embroidery stitches using crewels is a correctly termed crewel embroidery.

No design should be called a crewel pattern. The designs most commonly associated with crewel embroidery are Jacobean or Stuart (Early 17th century) because these fanciful and ornamental designs of East Indian influence were in vogue when this type of embroidery gained popularity during the 16th and 17th centuries with the invention of the steel needle. Crewel embroidery became more colorful during the 18th century with natural flower effects stitched in vivid hues and in more realistic patterns. Early American pieces were usually worked from English patterns but eventually Colonial needlewomen embroidered many original designs which have a simple, restrained yet unified style, much less repetitive in motif. Some beautiful embroideries have been created by modern designers who prefer the use of simplified or abstract form. It would, therefore, be correct to refer to a Jacobean design or an Early American design, etc., worked in crewel embroidery, but never to identify a work simply as a crewel design.

Most crewel embroidery is worked on linen which time and experience have proved to be most durable. While lovely effects have been produced on other materials, I recommend using only genuine crewels on good linen fabric when you are planning to create quality art pieces for heritage embroidery.

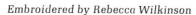

Embroidered by Rebecca Wilkinson

Embroidered by Grace O'Neil

Crewel embroidery adapts itself to beautiful detail as seen in this vase by Elsa S. Williams.

This dynamic arrangement of large, smooth petals and ribbon bow was created with the Long and Short stitch.

Detail of shading with the Long and Short stitch.

This clutch purse and Bermuda handbag were embroidered using a selection of only five stitches!

CHAPTER FOUR

How to begin

There are many excellent embroidery instructors conducting classes all over the United States. For the beginner this is undoubtedly the most helpful way to begin. The encouragement one receives from other members of the class is inspiring and rapidly increases one's confidence. However, when it is not possible to join such a group, it is possible to discover the art of embroidery by working directly from a good beginner's kit. I am constantly delighted with mail from women all over the country who write to tell me of the success they have achieved following the directions in my kits which they have purchased in their local needlework shops. The old adage "if you can read — you can cook," applies also to embroidery "if you can read — you can embroider."

Crewel embroidery sampler

Your first piece should be a small design so that you will soon experience the satisfaction of a completed project. Some teachers use a very complete stitch sampler for the beginner's first effort, since it offers a good opportunity to learn many stitches. This is a matter of personal choice. I prefer to limit the beginner to practice and use only five or six embroidery stitches at first and to doing these extremely well before going on to learn more. Complete directions for all the stitches, with detailed diagrams to illustrate them, are to be found in the glossary at the end of the book.

The sampler shown on page 28 is one I have found enjoyable because it teaches all the basic stitches while at the same time the embroiderer is producing a decorative box, pillow, or bookcover, for example. The finished sampler may, of course, also be worth dating and framing as a wall hanging.

Small embroideries like those on pages 33 and 34 are all good beginner's pieces. A few of these should be made before you attempt a larger project. If you haven't the courage to draw your own design, you can purchase these little motifs already printed on the fabric, in prepared kits. A good beginner's kit will include all the necessary materials and carefully diagrammed instructions with a stitch chart showing exactly how to form each type of stitch. Because crewel yarn handles well, and the colors blend so beautifully, you will discover much satisfaction in working your first piece in crewel.

Several interesting applications of the sampler.

Plate III   A BEGINNER'S PIECE.

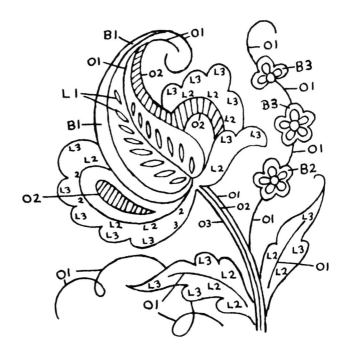

If you want to begin with the materials you have available, here is a little design that has many uses. You may frame it as a picture, use it on a pillow top, a bookcover, on a lampshade, pin cushion, box top, or on wearing apparel. The design is shown on page 34, decorating a stationery container.

1. Trace the design on transparent tracing paper with a medium hard pencil.

2. Transfer the traced design to the embroidery fabric using a non-smudging carbon paper. These plastic coated carbon sheets are available in office-supply stores. Use a medium lead pencil or metal stylus to press on the design. A soft pencil makes too broad a line and a hard, sharp lead will perforate or destroy the pattern. When you have a fairly distinct pattern on the cloth, it is helpful to go over the lines with a ballpoint laundry marking pen to establish permanent lines which will not rub off while you work.

3. Embroider the motif using crewel threads and a #3 crewel needle.

Stitch Key	*Color Key*
O = Outline	1 = Dark
B = Buttonhole	2 = Medium
L = Long and Short	3 = Light
F = French Knot	
D = Lazy Daisy	

Example: O1 indicates Outline stitch in the darkest shade. L3 indicates Long and Short stitch in the lightest shade.

Following the stitch and color keys you may now begin your embroidery.

A. The three lines of the main stem are embroidered in three shades of green Outline stitches. Here the Outline stitches are worked with the needle above the thread. This is called a _crewel outline_. When these three lines are completed you will notice that they blend, forming a solid area shaded from dark to light. (See page 62.)

B. Embroider the remaining scroll stems in dark green Outline stitches with the needle below the yarn. This is called the _stem outline_ and makes a very fine line which looks exactly like a thin stem. (See page 62.)
Have you noticed the difference in these two Outline stitches? In the first _crewel outline_ you can see every stitch while in the _stem outline_ it appears to have twisted, forming one single thread.

C. Embroider the fine Stem Outline on the lines in the center of the leaves.

D. The solid areas of the leaves are shaded in Long and Short stitches. See page 66 for instructions on Long and Short stitch.

E. Choose two colors which blend well together for the flowers. Blue and lavender tones are pleasant, or yellow and orange. The small flowers at the right are worked in _buttonhole_ stitches with _French Knot_ clusters in the center. Notice that the bottom flower is darker to create more interest on this side. If all three flowers were alike in tone the effect would be flat.

F. Use the Stem Outline stitch for the center line of the large flower with _lazy daisy_ stitches on each side of this line. The darker curved border which forms the center spray is worked by beginning at the top curve with a Crewel Outline which changes to a Buttonhole stitch when the area becomes wider. At the base of the center stem this line again becomes a Crewel Outline ending into the top curve area.

G. The latticed area on each side of this center form may be worked with flat _straight_ stitches which are outlined in Stem stitch.

H. All remaining areas of outside petals are worked in _long and short_ stitches.

When the piece is completed it is ready for blocking. (See Chapter 10.) Proper blocking produces a lovely raised effect and pulls the stitches into smooth, even areas while restoring the linen to its original weave. This cannot be done as effectively with a pressing iron.

Several small motifs suitable for beginners worked in crewel embroidery.

Articles decorated with small motifs worked in crewel embroidery.

Now that you have completed your first little piece you are ready to start your second. Perhaps you would like to try a pillow cover or a small picture. A handbag or sweater decoration can be very satisfying. These pieces when worked from kits will be embroidered with the same stitches you have already used in the beginner's piece and you can now introduce a few other basic stitches. If you are designing your own patterns, I urge you to keep the project simple and compatible with your skill. An elaborate design or a very large project confuses and discourages the inexperienced needleworker.

When you have completed two or three pieces and have learned to do Outline, Buttonhole, Long and Short, French Knots, Satin, Lazy Daisy, and Chain stitches, you will then be ready to begin a masterpiece. The Needlecraft House Masterpiece Collection consists of designs from museums, from outstanding embroidery designers including all the patterns of Louise Chrimes, and many of my own designs for embroidery. These printed linen pieces do not include directions and yarns. Instead they will permit you to choose your own stitches and your own selection of colors. You may choose a design which is the size and pattern suitable for a piece of furniture or to fit a lovely old picture frame.

Whenever I encourage an embroiderer to begin one of these Masterpiece Collection designs, I hasten to explain that we are not going to embroider the entire design at once. We only do one stem, one leaf, or one petal at a time. Consequently it is not at all difficult. There is tremendous personal satisfaction in working a piece which has not been diagrammed with pre-established stitches and colors.

First of all there is the satisfaction of choosing one's own colors. A chair seat, for example, could be worked in a monochromatic color scheme using four or five shades of one color. I have seen many handsome pieces worked in this way using all the hues of a color which exactly suited the room for which it was intended. The same chair seat could be done in two colors or in several colors to blend with an existing color scheme.

The second joy of working a piece which is not in kit form is the pleasure of utilizing the stitches one really enjoys doing. If you like to do French Knots you will, perhaps, work masses of them in some areas or if you prefer to keep the design more open and free you will then work the areas in simple lines.

The finished piece worked in this way will result in a completely original embroidery. It is not very likely that two people will produce exact duplicates. Their choice of colors and of stitches will result in a distinctly original, one-of-a-kind piece that has obviously more value than one which follows an established plan.

Pillow designed by Louise A. Chrimes.

Massed floral chair seat. A splendid example of the use of Long and Short stitches, designed by Louise A. Chrimes, and embroidered by Martha Hawes.

Elizabethan flowers. The original of this monochromatic embroidery was worked in five shades of rust-rose. Designed by the author, this was embroidered by Grace O'Neil.

When you have completed a few advanced pieces you are ready to participate in Heritage Embroidery. I urge you to direct your interests toward producing a piece that deserves to be displayed in a museum. A wing chair, a wall hanging, a sectional screen, draperies, and bed coverings are all desirable projects but small pieces can also be gems of needlework. To achieve museum quality, a piece should be made of good materials of lasting properties. It should be worked from a good design with carefully selected colors, but most important of all, it should be worked in excellent stitchery. One's tastes may differ in color and design, but excellence of workmanship is the prime factor of Heritage Embroidery.

Milford footstool. This design provides an opportunity for using interesting filling stitches. It is adapted from an old English pattern and was worked by the author.

Detail of an Elizabethan chair seat.

Curtain valance in a continuous-scroll border. Designed and embroidered by the author.

CHAPTER FIVE

Designing for embroidery

All fine art forms involve placing a design on a vacant area. The same factor applies to embroidery. Just as the blank canvas or paper confronts the fine painter, the linen or fabric in the same sense challenges the embroiderer. The texture of this background determines the design and materials to be used. A very fine weave of fabric will require a delicate design which can be worked best in fine embroidery threads. A rough textured, coarsely-woven fabric needs a larger, simplified pattern which adapts to heavy embroidery threads.

Before choosing the fabric it is wise to decide on the pattern or design to be embroidered. As in all art forms there is no limit to the variety of design which is applicable to embroidery. The design may reflect a period in history, it may be adapted from nature, or it may be entirely imaginative.

An infant's blanket with an interesting border design by the author, adaptable for use on sweaters. (From the Vogue Knitting Book, Special Issue for Children—Fall, 1964.)

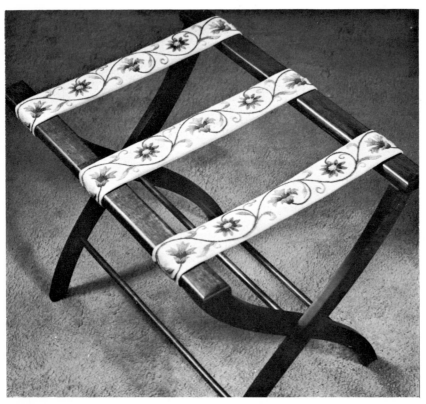

The author has designed these luggage-rack bands which may also be used as curtain tie-backs.

In embroidery the application of the design is of primary importance since the object to be decorated determines the type of design in most cases. It would, for example, be wrong to apply a modern abstract design on an Early American chair seat or a Jacobean design on a modern sling chair. Therefore, it is important to choose a pattern which compliments the furniture or the room where it is to be used. This also applies to wearing apparel where the embroidered design becomes a part of the garment.

When designing a pattern for embroidery it is important to have at least a basic knowledge of stitchery. Begin with free-flowing lines which can be executed with either Outline or Chain stitches. Then plan color areas which are to be worked in shaded Long and Short stitches or with interesting filling stitches. In addition to the areas to be embroidered it is necessary to remember that the fabric areas to be left uncovered are an integral part of the design and are also very important. These blank spaces should balance the design and be evenly distributed to avoid crowding which will produce disturbing solids or voids.

Symmetrical patterns are, perhaps, the easiest to design because they require planning only half or one fourth of the area. Symmetrical forms are used in many embroidery patterns because they create a well-balanced effect for bedspreads, pillows, curtains, and most rug designs. Examples of symmetrical patterns are shown below and in the sconces on page 16.

Spanish Riders. Designed by Louise A. Chrimes and embroidered by Elizabeth Schaff entirely in chain stitch with black yarn.

Suitable for pictures, pillows, or chair seats, these grape clusters were designed by the author and worked by Grace O'Neil.

This attractive arrangement of fruit is another central motif designed by the author and embroidered by June Clark.

Asymmetrical forms are not on opposite sides of an imaginary dividing line and therefore the design must create its own balance. This requires more drawing skill but allows for a freedom of form which adapts to any space. There is much satisfaction in this type of design because it has no measured restrictions. The pattern can freely reflect your interest in flowers, perhaps, which gives you an unlimited choice of color or it can be in decorative forms which might conform to the most exacting choice of materials.

When I begin an original design, I usually start with small thumbnail sketches. These little scribbles help me to decide upon the general shape of the design and the proposed area it is to cover. When my proposed layout has been generally arranged, I then frequently turn to a good reference for the details of the design. Photographs and picture books, magazines, greeting cards, and seed catalogs all provide good reference material for developing the drawing. The grape design on page 42 was requested by a woman who wanted to embroider fruit on the fabric of her dining-room chairs. The original, two-dimensional sketch was easy to plan for the area given, but my grapes were flat and not realistic enough in color. Fortunately, I found an advertisement for grape juice which pictured some luscious grapes in deep purple tones and there I conveniently had an excellent reference to help me improve the color and form in the design. Using extraneous sources of reference material is especially helpful when embroidering flowers.

Personalized designs which tell a story require even more particular reference sources. This is essential when designing a family tree or coat-of-arms. I have seen maps and manuscripts worked in embroidery stitches as well as portraits and scenes. Some of these subjects can be developed by mechanically enlarging the original with a pantograph or by having a photograph enlarged, but it is important to simplify or cartoon the design so that it can be adapted to workable embroidery.

The great Tree of Life is perhaps the best known and most popular crewel embroidery design. The study of its history reveals that much of the elaborate, early embroidery, just as in painting, was worked for ecclesiastical use with religious symbols heavily dominant in the majority of designs. When the use of secular design was advanced it was natural that the Tree of Life would become one of its first forms. There is no limit to its interpretations. Massive tree trunks with elaborately curling leaves and fantastic flowers were embroidered during the 17th century by English needleworkers. The New England embroideress adapted the Tree of Life to the simple openwork forms which we associate with American Colonial design. The 20th century has borrowed liberally from the past and combined the grace of openwork with the strength of elaborate form and produced some very beautiful Tree of Life designs.

The progress of American embroidery in recent years is due in large measure to Louise A. Chrimes (1872-1963) who devoted her life to designing and teaching Heritage Embroidery. During the machine age when fine hand embroidery was largely neglected, the art was kept alive by Mrs. Chrimes and her associates. Her designs adapted the best forms of the old patterns to tasteful and carefully proportioned, even-flowing forms which are the delight of the modern needlewoman. She is identified with many Tree of Life patterns which are beautifully balanced, have smooth-flowing lines and carefully-drawn flowers and leaves. I am very fortunate indeed, to have been selected to perpetuate the enormous legacy of her designs and many of them are included in these pages.

Frequently, enthusiasts adapt their patterns from the original designs of a master embroiderer or from museum pieces. I regret to say that many of these adaptations have distorted the original patterns because the embroiderer copied poorly or because he neglected to correct or improve the design after it was drawn. To make a working design for Heritage Embroidery I urge you to give as much thought to the drawing as you will apply to the embroidery. The tool called a _French curve_, which can be purchased at any art supply shop, is a most useful aid in drawing perfectly formed curves, and to keep a clean surface on your paper when correcting the drawings repeatedly, a kneaded eraser is essential.

Tree of Life, one of the lovely designs always associated with the gifted, creative needleworker, Louise A. Chrimes. Embroidered by Grace O'Neil.

A fine example of a graceful Tree of Life form designed by Louise Chrimes and embroidered by Thelma McAlpine.

Following is a step-by-step sample correction and improvement of a simple embroidery motif. Most designs will generally need to be handled in this way. These suggestions should help you to produce some lovely embroideries which are well-designed, and therefore, easily worked.

Illustration A

This design was traced from an original without making any corrections. At first glance it appears to be a simple, easy-to-embroider pattern which is suitable for many small items. The embroiderer who is conscious of good design should, however, have immediately noticed the many imperfections in this pattern and quickly thought about improving it.

Illustration B

This is the same design with stems in much better proportion and in the right places. The scroll at lower left is balanced in the area and three round forms make a better, less crowded arrangement than the four which originally appeared in A. The leaves have been improved and the berries at the top are properly placed with stems that seem to grow more naturally. The leaves on the higher flower are in better proportion. The large blossom at the lower right allows more even spacing for rows of Chain or Buttonhole stitches, while the scroll line in back of it has improved its direction.

Illustration C

Because design B has two green leaves on one side and two major flowers on the opposite side of the arrangement, it would not allow for a pleasant distribution of color. Therefore, I have now changed the large leaf to a flower and have also added a leaf at the lower left to balance the other green leaves. Changing the center circles of the five-petal flower makes it more interesting and the heavier stem strengthens this blossom in the design.

C

The placement of the design is not a serious matter when centering a motif on a chair seat or pillow. However, the placement of a design on a large wall panel or drapery is a very important part of the design. Borders must be carefully balanced with generous, well-proportioned margins. When positioning a large design on a panel, the areas at sides and top should be equal but the bottom space should be wider. The same proportions apply when cutting a mat for framing the completed piece. There are exceptions to this rule which should be considered when placing an unbalanced pattern, but traditional designs will usually require these proportions.

In Heritage Embroidery the design is of great importance. While the embroiderer deserves credit for her work and has the right to include her initials on the pieces, it is nevertheless important to mention the original designer's name when exhibiting the finished piece publicly. If the design is adapted from a museum piece, formal credit should properly be given to this source of the design.

At left, an old hearth-bench design. Embroidered by Mrs. Edward Harding, this is reproduced with the courtesy of her daughter, Mrs. J. B. Richmond of Dover, Massachusetts.

Adapted from Mrs. Harding's hearth bench, this crewel embroidered piano-bench cover below was stitched by Grace O'Neil.

CHAPTER SIX

Color in needlework

The excitement of color is perhaps the greatest joy for the modern embroiderer. To choose a color scheme for a design is one of my greatest pleasures. Modern dyeing methods provide us with so many shades and colors, I frequently wonder what it must have been like when embroiderers had to dye their own threads with berry juice and tree bark. Today it is possible to make an unlimited choice of color schemes by using many hues of one color or by combining several shades of different colors.

Traditional designs should, of course, be worked in traditional colors. The old crewel embroidery patterns which have been copied for generations would lose their charm if they were worked in bold unrelated colors. Careful attention to the harmony of colors must also apply to ecclesiastical embroidery. The church which has stained glass windows requires deep reds and purples while one with clear glass windows will need blues, greens, and pastel shades. It is, therefore, very important to choose colors which blend with the established interior since strong contrasts should never occur in this type of embroidery.

The greatest freedom of color is allowed when the color scheme is to reflect one's personal taste. Here the vivacious individual may use vibrant tones of color, the delicate feminine personality may lean toward pastel tones in her work, the conservative person often chooses muted colors and the nature lover will select her palette from the flowers of the garden, balanced with the natural greens.

When the colors are chosen according to both the design and the personal taste of the embroiderer, the next step is to arrange these together to obtain the best possible artistic effect. When several colors are employed it is important to arrange them to create a good balance. Avoid using too many of the same colors in one area or on two motifs which are to appear at the same eye level. Light tones of a color usually are arranged at the top since sunlight and most artificial light comes from above. To create proper shading the light source must also be directed from one side as you work. A right-handed person sits with the light at his left, while a left-handed person works best with the light source at the right. Consequently, if you are right handed you will arrange your colors to be darker in the lower areas on the right sides of the design. Many embroiderers who have had no art instruction create flat designs with no effect of depth. This, of course, is the result of choosing the wrong tones of color.

The history of needlework reveals that many professional embroiderers were men. The Worshipful Company of Broderers, in England, received its first charter on October 25, 1561. By 1634 the Broderers were faced with competition from private domestic production and from a considerable output by nuns before the Reformation. For want of employment, a great part of the Company were "constrained to become porters, water bearers, and the like." Since color blindness is more prevalent among men than women, it is interesting to discover that most monochromatic pieces in English embroidery were worked during the period prior to 1700 and during the time when the professionals were chiefly men.

Monochromatic embroidery worked completely in one color eliminates the problems of color layout. But, since it uses several shades of the same

Three versions of the famous Duxbury Scroll designed by Louise A. Chrimes. This beautiful, flowing pattern is shown left, on a sweater border; above, decorating a pillow; and on page 54, as a chair seat. It is really an excellent pattern for monochromatic embroidery.

color, it provides, nevertheless, good opportunity for dimensional effects created by the arrangement of light and dark tones. Some of the most beautiful pieces I have ever seen have been worked in monochromatic colors.

A real satisfaction can be obtained from working with one family of colors. This is especially advantageous for the beginner who needs to concern herself with improving her stitchery. A design worked in five tones of one color can be an exciting experience of shading from light to dark.

Interior designers are especially fond of monochromatic embroideries because they can more easily be blended with any room decoration. Multicolored embroideries sometimes can create a disturbance in a room which is planned for limited color or unusual color effects. The monochromatic piece can be worked in shades of a color that will suit or exactly match other fabrics, carpeting, or wall decorations.

	1-1
	1-2
	1-3
	1-4
	1-5

1-1
1-2
1-3
1-4
1-5

7-1
7-2
7-3
7-4
7-5

14-1
14-2
14-3
14-4
14-5

21-1
21-2
21-3
21-4
21-5

2-1
2-2
2-3
2-4
2-5

8-1
8-2
8-3
8-4
8-5

15-1
15-2
15-3
15-4

22-1
22-2
22-3
22-4
22-5

3-1
3-2
3-3
3-4
3-5

9-1
9-2
9-3
9-4
9-5

16-1
16-2
16-3
16-4
16-5

23-1
23-2
23-3
23-4
23-5

4-1
4-2
4-3
4-4
4-5

10-1
10-2
10-3
10-4
10-5

17-1
17-2
17-3
17-4

24-1
24-2
24-3
24-4
24-5

5-1
5-2
5-3
5-4
5-5

11-1
11-2
11-3
11-4

18-1
18-2
18-3
18-4
18-5

25-1
25-2
25-3
25-4

6-1
6-2
6-3
6-4
6-5

12-1
12-2
12-3
12-4
12-5

19-1
19-2
19-3
19-4

26-1
26-2
26-3
26-4

5000

13-1
13-2
13-3
13-4

20-1
20-2
20-3
20-4

27-1
27-2
27-3
27-4
27-5

Because of the great renewal of interest in Old English and Early American embroideries, many needleworkers are now using dull color tones for antique effects. These colors then achieve the faded appearance to resemble the present condition of the antique pieces which are being copied. When I visited the textile director of a museum in London she seemed surprised and concerned that American embroiderers were anxious to copy work in old, faded colors. She revealed to me the bright original colors on the reverse side of some of the old embroideries and explained that these old pieces have now reached maximum fading. To copy these faded colors with modern fast-color yarns will no doubt produce pleasant antique effects which will last for many years. However, as a precaution against the fading effects of sunlight and fluorescent lighting I believe it is quite important to choose colors which are somewhat brighter than the very old ones. It would be a disaster to copy faded colors which may result in sad gray tones a hundred years from now.

True colors are seldom used in Heritage Embroidery. This is, perhaps, because these bold strong tones are not harmonious to most surroundings. When we refer to true colors we mean the bright clear red, orange, yellow,

The central motif from the cover of a piano bench, primarily using Long and Short stitches, is adapted from an American design combining animal and plant forms. This was embroidered by Grace O'Neil.

The Tree of Enchantment is a delightful embroidery for a child's room. Designed and embroidered by Grace O'Neil.

Squirrel and pinecones worked primarily in Outline stitch, with Long and Short stitch on the squirrel's body and Tufted stitch for the tail. Designed by Daphne Kennedy, it was embroidered by June Clark.

This Squirrel in a Chestnut Tree was also designed by Daphne Kennedy and worked by June Clark.

green, blue, and violet you carefully put on paper squares as a child to identify the spectrum. These bold colors are frequently used to embroider military emblems or flags and pennants where contrast is more important than color harmony.

Natural colors include all the tones we find in trees, flowers, earth, sky, and sea. These colors hold a great fascination for embroiderers who enjoy recreating natural forms and they adapt well to decoration on wearing apparel. As in nature, there is no limit to the shadings of natural colors. Consider the palest pink in a rose and the deepest red, or the light lavender of lilac and the dark purple anemone. All these and many more have a cleanliness of color which does not include any grayness of tone.

The range of a color from light to dark in several different tone steps of the same color relates the lightest to the darkest. This is, therefore, called a family of colors. When an embroiderer refers to a family of blues, for example, this could be true blue, gray blue, green blue, or lavender blue. While it is possible to blend a family of true colors with a family of natural colors, it is not a good relation of colors to mix true colors with antique colors. The mixture becomes a harsh contrast and is disturbing to the eye. For best results choose families which are related closely to each other.

The color plate on page 55 shows 27 families of colors which are available in crewel yarn. These colors have all been selected to amply provide beautiful color schemes for Heritage Embroidery.

An example of many colors blended within a small design area to achieve the effect of depth.

CHAPTER SEVEN

Three important stitches

The study of embroidery stitches is a fascinating adventure. I am constantly amazed, however, to meet expert needlewomen who do not completely understand the basic embroidery stitches and who also claim to despair of ever conquering their struggles with the Long and Short stitch.

I do not believe it is at all important to know how to do every embroidery stitch. Some of the most beautiful embroideries are worked completely in only three or four stitches. A sampler of many kinds of stitches would be fun to do and a good reference for teachers, but I am always appalled to see a lovely design massacred by a confusion of dozens of different stitches which looks in effect, like a practice piece.

If you are interested in learning many stitches, I would like to refer you to Jacqueline Enthoven's book, "The Stitches of Creative Embroidery," published in 1964 by the Reinhold Publishing Company. This book contains easy-to-follow directions and diagrams for over 200 stitches. It is an excellent reference book to have in your personal library.

The following are three of the most important and basic stitches: the Outline, French Knot and Long and Short stitches. They are absolutely essential in crewel work. When you have mastered these you can proceed to embroider with confidence, with more ease and personal pleasure. Perhaps you have been taught to do these stitches in exactly the same way that I have. However, I have met many teachers who do not really know the proper use of the three basic outline stitches, and therefore, I always like to begin by explaining them again just to be sure they are understood.

OUTLINE STITCHES

Work from left to right with the thread toward you and the needle stitching into the guide line to be embroidered. Every stitch touches the previous stitch and on the reverse side you will form a perfect row of Back stitches. You will discover that every stitch remains clearly visible. This Outline stitch may be worked in rows to create a solid, even-textured mass, or shaded area. Try this using crewel yarn and you will see how beautifully the rows blend together. This is therefore, called the _Crewel Outline_ stitch.

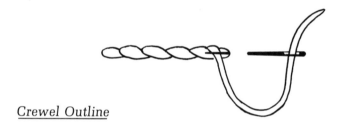

Crewel Outline

Now try the same stitch again but keep the thread on the other side of the needle, away from you. You will soon discover that your stitches twist to form what appears to be one straight and continuous long stem without noticeable separate stitches. This is, of course, the _Stem Outline_ and is principally used for fine stems and thin outlining.

Stem Outline

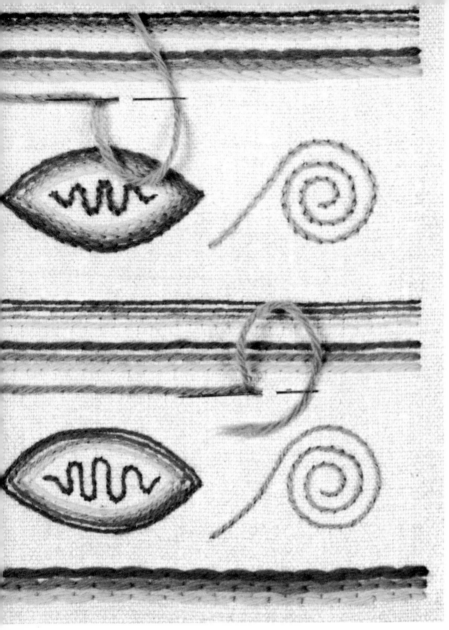

Outline Stitches

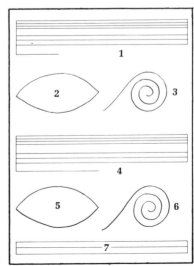

Key to Outline Stitches

The third outline stitch is called an *Alternating Outline*. First the thread is held on one side of the needle, toward you; the next stitch will have the thread on the other side of the needle, away from you. Continue alternating the thread with every stitch to produce this lumpy, coarse outline which is excellent for forming heavier stems or for framing borders. Evenly spaced, Alternating Outline stitches are sometimes used as a base for twisting a contrasting thread around it.

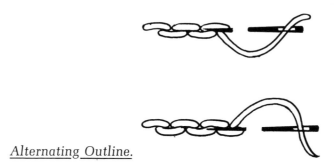

Alternating Outline.

The photograph opposite, shows the three outline stitches in various arrangements.

Sections #1, #2, and #3 were worked in Crewel Outline stitch with the needle on the line and the thread below the needle. Notice that every stitch shows and yet the lines blend together. It is important to notice, however, that the curved lines in #2 do not hold a perfect line with this Crewel Outline stitch.

Sections #4, #5, and #6 were worked in Stem Outline with the needle on the line and the thread above the needle. Here you will notice that the stitches form a solid line and they do not blend into each other. The lines of Section #6 and the center of Section #5 remain firm and smooth.

The Crewel Outline and the Stem Outline patterns shown here were worked both in crewel yarn and a heavier tapestry yarn. The stitches were kept the same size to show you what a difference occurs when the thread is held above or below the needle. The three lines of Section #7 at the bottom of this page are worked in Alternating Outline stitches.

Do not use an embroidery hoop when making Outline stitches and remember to keep the thread relaxed so that the material does not pucker.

FRENCH KNOTS.

The French Knot is one of my favorite stitches. It is beautiful for textured effects, for flower centers, for shading large and small areas. In fact it can be the principal stitch for some designs. Unfortunately, many embroiderers shy away from this stitch because they have had poor results with it. I have seen many embroideries which were otherwise well done but the French Knots were lumpy and irregular. I hope you will try my method and find it helpful. If you have been doing this stitch in a different way, this may seem awkward at first but a little practice will result in perfect knots which have a dimple in the middle.

Bring needle and thread up at point where knot is to be made. Hold thread with left thumb and forefinger about two inches away from the cloth and keep the thread taut. With right hand twist the _needle_ once around the thread in a clockwise motion. Then lock the twist in place by pulling the taut thread under the point of the needle. Insert needle into fabric as closely as possible to the spot where the thread emerges (but not in the same hole) and pull threaded needle to wrong side of the embroidery. See Glossary of Stitches for diagram of French Knots.

For all fine embroidery and especially in crewel embroidery, it is important to turn the needle only _once_ around the yarn. This will keep an even surface to your work. It is especially important when embroidering chair seats or items that will receive surface wear, to avoid making any high knots which will wear off while the remainder of the embroidery remains in good condition. If larger knots are desired for creative stitchery, use a heavier yarn or several strands of thread in the needle, but remember to wind only once to make the perfect knot which has a dimple in the middle.

As soon as you have achieved perfect knots without tails or loops, your attention should be directed to deliberately spacing the knots to produce an even surface. This can be accomplished by bringing the needle and thread up through the fabric one knot's distance away from each previous knot, turn the needle around the yarn and insert the needle point close to the previous knot. This procedure will resemble that of a Backstitch and result in more evenly-spaced knots.

The illustration on page 65 will show you some lovely effects obtained with French Knots. This stitch can be used to cover large areas as well as for fine lines. Line #1 across the top shows a row of single French Knots worked in heavier yarn. The berries in cluster #2 show a smooth rounded effect as does the orange in #5 which was worked in several shades of one color. The filled

French Knots. Various effects achieved using the French Knot.

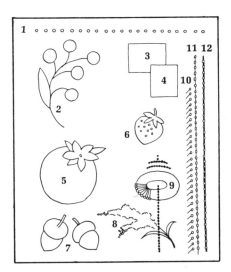

Key to French Knots

areas of #3 and #4 are examples of the use of French Knots alone and in combination with an Outline stitch to create an overall effect. The seeded textural effect of the strawberry, #6, was obtained by closely grouping small French Knots in shades of bright red, adding a few light-colored knots to make it look realistic. The acorns of #7 develop a three-dimensional effect when the French Knot caps are seen in contrast to the smoothly-stitched lower part of the nut. The goldenrod blossoms in #8 were created by loosely arranging knots to produce the soft characteristic effect of this flower. The lines of #9 were made of a firm row of small knots spaced very closely together. The oval form of this design consists of French Knots sewn down on the outside line with the needle emerging at the inside line of the oval. This same form of French Knot is shown in lines #10 and #11. Line #10 has the thread emerging from the left and the knot is placed at an angle upward and to the right. Line #11 has the knot placed a short distance above the emerging thread to form a continuous line. The back of the work will appear to be a row of Outline stitches. Line #12 was made by sewing a line of Chain stitches. A French Knot was then sewed over the spot where each link of the chain was formed.

Use an embroidery hoop for working all French Knots.

LONG AND SHORT STITCH

A whole book could be written about the Long and Short stitch. Most embroiderers need help with this stitch but once they have mastered it, it becomes their greatest achievement and the stitch they will use more than any other. There is great satisfaction for the needleworker who sees a leaf or flower petal come to life with the lovely shaded effects she has produced with this stitch. More difficult, perhaps, is the shading of an animal or bird form but since this stitch can reproduce the texture of feathers and animal fur it is almost always used for these motifs.

There are several methods for working Long and Short stitch. Just as most artists have their own techniques to develop their own style, the skilled embroiderer finds her own best method for working the Long and Short stitch. It may be smooth and even-textured with lovely gradations of color or it may be bold and rough-textured with accents and highlights added as the work progresses. The most complicated method is to use several needles threaded with various shades of yarn, all in work at the same time rather than finishing all of one shade before proceding to the next. This technique produces both shading and contrast in a continuous, smooth stitch effect.

Long and Short Stitches

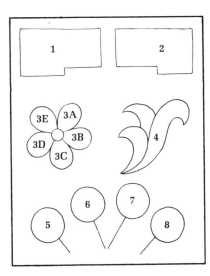

Key to Long and Short Stitches.

67

Regardless of which method you choose to develop, it is important to re-member that the Long and Short stitches appear _only around the outside edge_ of the design. All the stitches in the center are long, straight stitches. Consider the corner of a brick chimney or a wall foundation: You will remember that the half brick and the whole brick at the end set up the spacing of all the whole bricks in the middle section. It is the same with the Long and Short stitch. The pattern begins on the outside edge of the design with a long stitch, then a stitch next to it which is half as long as the long stitch, another long stitch, a short stitch, a long stitch, etc. (For practice work try making your long stitch one-half inch long and your short stitch one-quarter inch long.) The second row and all succeeding rows will be all long stitches.

Begin the second row by stitching up into the thread of the tip of the previous short stitches. Do not stitch into the previous long stitches. The third row of stitches should similarly join into the long stitches of the first row. Now you will find that you have established the pattern of staggered, evenly-spaced stitches. At the end of the area you will need a few short stitches to fill in and finish the remaining space. See the stitches photographed across the top of the illustration on page 67. The spacing of the stitch is clearly seen in this flat area. Section #1 was worked in tapestry yarn to show the effect obtained with heavier thread. Section #2 is shown using fine crewel yarn which permits the use of many more threads and thereby, more color and more stitches, to blend in the area.

Floral Wreath. An excellent example of the use of Long and Short stitches. The design is by Louise A. Chrimes and it was embroidered by Marion Mossman.

Detail of the Floral
Wreath.

Most beginners find it difficult to achieve the right direction for their stitches. My solution to this problem is to stitch up into the work and lay the thread forward in the direction I want it to go, then stitch down into the linen. If you are embroidering a flower petal for example, this will always help you to aim toward the base of the petal or the center of the flower if you begin from the outside edge. Notice the flower, #3, on page 67. Turning clockwise, petal 3A shows only the outside, first row. Petal 3B shows two rows of stitches. Petal 3C includes a few more stitches of the same middle color. Petal 3D has a row of dark threads and petal 3E shows the petal completed with all stitches going in the same direction—aimed toward the center of the flower.

The direction in which stitches are sewed in Long and Short stitch creates many unusual effects and lovely shading. Notice the curved scroll leaf, form #4, on page 67. All the stitches begin at the top of each section and end at the bottom point. Stitching up into the thread and down into the cloth will create a smooth effect without needle holes or lumpy areas. Remember to

Another example of crewel embroidery detail, done by the author.

keep your thread soft and relaxed so that the next shade or color will blend smoothly into the previous work. Stitching up into the previous row will fluff up the previous stitch and keep the texture even. Occasionally you may wish to raise a petal or a leaf so that it remains in the foreground. This is accomplished by sewing a row of Split stitches on the outside line before beginning the Long and Short stitches. The first row of Long and Short stitches is worked over the line of Split stitches to create a slightly raised effect and a very smooth edge.

The four small circles at the bottom of the page are all exactly the same size since they were traced around the edge of a twenty-five cent piece. Circle #5 appears to be wider because the stitches are worked horizontally. In #6 the stitches are arranged vertically and it appears to be taller. The wheel effect of #7 was created by aiming all the stitches toward the center of the circle. And in #8 the wheel was developed into an interesting pattern by using contrasting shades in a symmetrical form.

All the many effects of these designs, worked in basic Long and Short stitch have innumerable variations which you will develop as you work up subsequent pieces.

After you have mastered this first method of embroidering the Long and Short stitch you will want to attempt another method. To achieve a brush stroke technique, the experienced needle artist works all dark areas first. The second tone of color is added next, etc., until all shades are worked in, saving the lightest to use last for highlights. With this method the stitches may vary in length and are not expected to be evenly spaced. (See rabbit on page 73.) The stitch technique is also different because smoothness must be achieved by fitting stitches between other stitches and no attempt is made to keep even rows. You will be able to create fascinating needle paintings with this method of using the Long and Short stitch.

The most difficult technique of working Long and Short stitch, as I have mentioned, is the multi-needle method. This is used primarily in portrait work and for embroidering animal fur. By threading several needles in a variety of shades and colors you can work in one smooth direction changing the color with each stitch to achieve the desired effect. The needles not in use are simply kept hanging on the underside of your work. (See fawn at lower left of page 73.) This creature was worked beginning at the nose and ending at the feet using five needles threaded with five shades of brown.

All Long and Short stitches should be worked using a hoop with the fabric stretched taut and the hoop screwed securely.

Key to Plate V.

CHAPTER EIGHT

Inspirations

All embroiderers, just as other artists, require inspiration and research material. The fine needlework displayed at museums and exhibitions is the very best source of ideas for the serious embroiderer. He or she will be encouraged to do better work and, in addition, will benefit by these museum trips with new ideas in the potential use of stitches.

The following projects present suggestions which may be adapted to your own designs.

ANIMALS

A. *Leaping Hound*   This dog is worked completely in Split stitch. Begin with the darkest color as your guide and gradually shade to light as you work in rows of Split stitches.

B. *Donkey*   Start with fine Stem Outline of entire figure. Work each tone area in flat Satin stitch.

C. *Goat*   Complete outline in Stem stitch. Horns, ear, beard in Stem stitch; hooves, nose, and eye in Satin stitches. Couched Trellis fills in the entire body area.

Plate V ANIMALS. →

D. *Reclining Fawn*   Multi-needle Long and Short stitches. See page 71 for details. Begin at nose and work toward the feet.

E. *Lamb*   Using French Knots start at outside edges, work inward. Use shading to create a wooly effect. Add details in Straight stitches.

F. *Leaping Deer*   With basic Long and Short stitches, beginning at his back work stitches neatly downward to simulate the deer's pelt. Dark accents and shadows are added last.

G. *Rabbit*   Brush stroke Long and Short stitch "paints" the rabbit. Work all dark accents first, ending with highlights.

H. *Squirrel*   Long and Short stitch is used starting at the back and working to the squirrel's underside. Accent legs with a few rows of Split stitches. The fluffy effect of the tail is achieved with the Tufted stitch.

STEMS AND TREE TRUNKS

A. Three Buttonhole stitches grouped together will form a shell. This stem was embroidered in two colors. With the first color embroider buttonhole shells on one side of the stem. Fit shells of a second color into the first, stitching along the opposite side.

B. The shading of this gracefully curved stem was achieved with four rows of Crewel Outline stitch in four shades of green.

C. When you examine this complicated stem you will find that the two dark brown lines are simple Stem Outline stitches. Between these there is a repeat border of XIIIXIII worked in green Buttonhole stitches. On the outside edge along the right side are light green Buttonhole stitches spaced widely apart. Diagonally from tip to base is a Straight stitch in light brown. This same color in Stem stitch forms a row to complete the center of the stem.

D. This handsome tree trunk has appeared in several of my embroideries because I enjoy doing it. The rows of Chain stitches which set the pattern must be small and evenly spaced. The filling stitches are inserted into the chain along the outside edge to create a rounded, lifted edge but in the center area the long horizontal stitches are placed over and under the chain to create a basket effect.

E. This fine, smooth curve is in Stem Outline stitch. Two shades of brown create the dimensional effect when the lighter scroll passes over the darker curve.

F. Three rows of Chain stitches in three shades of green.

G. A Herringbone-stitch center has a row of Stem Outline stitch on each side.

H. Coral stitches in two shades of brown.

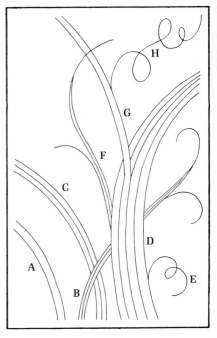

Key to Plate VI. *(page 76)*.

Plate VI   TREE TRUNK AND STEMS.   ➤

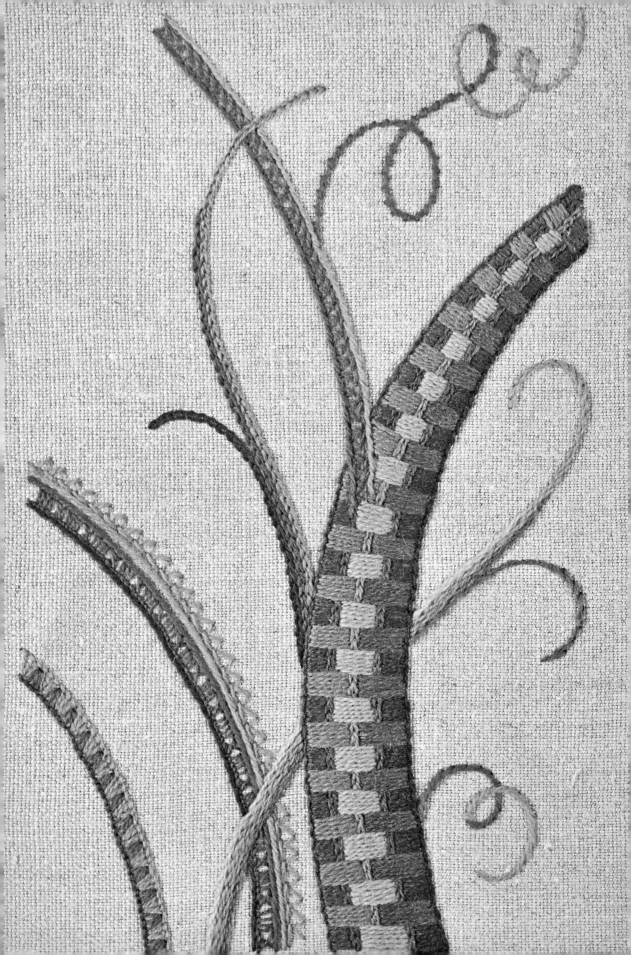

LEAVES

A. Here are five easy ways to embroider the same leaf:

Starting at the tip work in Long and Short stitch ending with the dark Stem Outline stitch.

Work Long and Short stitches from outside edge of leaf to converge at the center vein. The leaf will appear realistically indented.

Left half of the leaf is in closely placed Buttonhole stitch; the other side is worked in Herringbone with fine Stem Outline.

Chain stitch using darkest color is begun at outside edges, worked inward to lightest color in even, curved rows.

Double Satin stitch beginning at point of leaf and ending with short Stem Outline.

B. All lines are in fine Stem Outline stitch with center loops worked in Lazy Daisy stitch.

C. Smooth Long and Short stitches in three shades of green with center vein indented as in the second leaf in group A.

D. Worked in brush stroke Long and Short stitches with indented center vein as in the second leaf of group A.

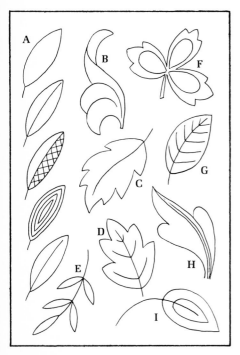

Key to Plate VII (*page 77*).

← Plate VII   LEAVES.

E. Smooth Long and Short stitches in three shades of green worked from light to dark ending with a dark green stem in Crewel Outline.

F. Begin with closely-spaced Couched Trellis stitch center. Finish with neatly worked outside Buttonhole edge.

G. Worked in vertical Laid stitches across entire leaf surface. Fine Stem stitch outline is embroidered curving across and *on top of* the Laid stitches.

H. Solid area in three shades of green Crewel Outline stitches. Right and left edges in Chain stitch. Left center in a shaded mass of Seed stitches. Right side area in tiny Cross Stitch filling.

I. Fine Stem Outline with Herringbone-stitch filling.

FLOWERS

A. *Red Bee Balm*   Flower, stem, and leaves are completely worked in rows of Crewel Outline stitches.

B. *Pink Rose*   The flower is in basic Long and Short stitch with a Split stitch under the lifted petal edges. The stem is in Stem Outline. Leaves are in brush stroke Long and Short.

C. *Yellow Yarrow*   Masses of French Knots form the blossoms. Stem Outline was used for the stems. Lazy Daisy stitches have a Single stitch in the center to form the leaves. These Single stitches are of a deeper shade than the loop.

D. *Blue Iris*   Flower is worked in basic Long and Short. A few yellow French Knots give realistic texture to the yellow area of the large drooping petal. Notice the spiral effect on the bud by using stitch direction to best advantage. Leaves are in basic Long and Short. Stems in Crewel Outline.

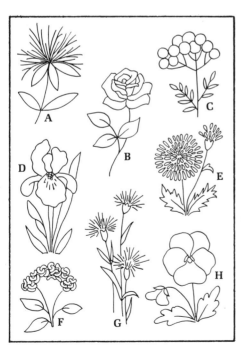

Key to Plate VIII.

E. *Orange Chrysanthemum*	Masses of Lazy Daisy stitches in orderly progressive arrangement have a Single stitch of a deeper shade in the center of each loop. Stem Outline is used for the stems. The leaves are in Long and Short with dark accents added as surface stitches.
F. *Red Cockscomb*	The top of the blossom is embroidered in masses of realistically curved Bullion stitches. The lower section is shaded in basic Long and Short. Leaves are in Double Satin stitches and short stems are Crewel Outline.
G. *Blue Cornflowers*	The flowers are worked in Single stitches. Leaves are Split stitches. Stems are in Stem Outline. A few Long and Short stitches create the shading at the base of the flower.
H. *Purple Pansy*	Hidden Split stitches are sewn around petal edges to pad them so they appear to be raised. Long and Short stitches were worked over these Split stitches in brush stroke technique. Two light Bullion stitches with a dark yellow accent between them form the pollen center. Smooth Stem Outline stitches form the stems. Basic Long and Short is used for the leaves.

CHAPTER NINE

finishing

Every piece of finished embroidery needs to be blocked. Whenever possible, avoid using an iron. Even a good steam iron cannot realign the fabric weave to its original shape. Proper blocking can do this and it also will raise and enrich your embroidery instead of flattening it.

HOW TO MAKE A BLOCKING BOARD

For best results make your blocking board base from a piece of insulation board. The cellulose type is best because pins and staples can be inserted and removed easily. Do not use any wooden board, plywood, or plasterboard. Your lumber dealer or hardware supplier has insulated wallboard in sheets four-by-eight feet. Ask him to cut it to the sizes you need. One sheet will provide you with the following desirable sizes: 4' x 4', 2' x 4', and two cut 2' x 2'. You will be able to block hundreds of pieces on these sections, using them over and over again.

A blocking board showing embroidery tacked right-side-down to the mounting cloth.

Careful blocking preserved the stitch
texture and even fabric-weave of this
piece. (Detail.)

The wallboard should be covered with clean, heavy white muslin or drill cloth similar to that used for ironing-board covers. With a staple gun, tack down the cover around the outside edge making certain that the cloth is pulled taut. This must be done with care because this fabric will be permanently attached to the board. If you do not have a staple gun you can use rust-free thumb-tacks. Dampen entire cloth lightly with a wet sponge to shrink the fabric so it is really tight across the board. Dry thoroughly.

Using a laundry-marking pen and a ruler draw a horizontal line across the center of the fabric-covered board. Using a triangle or compass draw a vertical line, dividing the board exactly into fourths. Keeping the lines at right angles, add parallel crosslines two inches apart until the entire board is cov-

ered in two-inch squares. These lines will be your guide lines for blocking various sizes of finished embroideries time after time. This permanent blocking board should be stored with cloth attached.

HOW TO BLOCK DRY

If your embroidery has not been soiled you will want to block it dry. With *right side of embroidery face down* on the blocking board arrange the piece with linen threads running parallel to the pencil lines of the board. Pin corners temporarily for position. Staple or tack one side of the piece following a guide line, pulling the fabric flat and smooth at the same time. Tack the op-

This massive flower arrangement was blocked several times while it was being embroidered. (Detail.)

posite side in the same way, this time pulling the fabric smooth but not too tight. Tack the remaining two sides, beginning at the middle working outward to the corners until all edges are firm and smoothly applied. Remove temporary pins at corners.

With a damp sponge or a clean damp cloth, wet the entire embroidery fabric. Be sure to thoroughly and evenly moisten both the fabric and the embroidery. Allow to dry for twenty-four hours before removing your embroidery from the board.

HOW TO BLOCK WET

When embroidery work has been soiled from handling, it is best to launder the piece before blocking. Squeeze dry but do not wring it out. Remove any excess moisture by rolling it in absorbent toweling before tacking it to the board. Follow the same directions as for dry-blocking but here re-wetting, of course, will not be necessary after tacking it to the board.

All blocking should be done with the embroidery placed face down on the blocking cloth so that stitches are not disturbed nor rubbed with the sponge. The mounting cloth and porous cellulose board will absorb some moisture and provide air-drying on both sides of the piece at the same time.

When moistening very large pieces the edges should first be well-dampened on all four sides to avoid shrinking in any one direction. Continue moistening toward the center of the piece. Since large projects absorb more water and become heavy, it is best to dry them in a horizontal position. If this is not possible, be sure to reverse the upright board during the first hour so that all edges can dry evenly and water marks are avoided.

This excellent method of blocking can be used for all wool embroidery and for needlepoint. It is, of course, not practical to block most wearing apparel. For garments and extremely large items such as bedspreads and draperies, we do suggest pressing on the wrong side with a steam iron rather than pinning to a blocking board. Place turkish toweling under the piece, with the embroidery face down. Do not allow the full weight of the iron to fall on the embroidery as it will crease the wool fibrils of the thread and create distortion in the stitches.

Crewel embroidery yarn
worked on linen twill.

CHAPTER TEN   *Materials and tools*

The craftsman who is interested in heritage embroidery must also be concerned about choosing the best materials and tools for her work. Just as a painter needs the finest brushes and canvas and smoothly-ground pigments to produce his best painting, the needle artist who plans to produce beautiful embroideries must be sure to have the best supplies.

The test of time has proved linen to be one of the most durable fabrics and excellent for embroidery. Perhaps some of the new synthetic fibers will prove to be as durable but, unfortunately, many do not hold stitches as securely as does linen. When embroidering on linen you will find that your embroidery threads will not slip out of place or disturb any previous stitches. Long, strong, flax fibres permit you to stitch directly into a thread without disturbing the basic weave as happens with cotton fabric. Therefore, I strongly recommend using linen for all crewel embroidery.

Embroidery linen is available in square weave and twill. The twill weave resembles serge and is the most durable fabric for chair seats and upholstery. The diagonal wale of the linen twill is usually not noticeable in the cloth, making it appear to be a solid fabric without texture. Therefore, it serves as an excellent background for all embroidery. Very firm twill with fine threads should be embroidered with a finer needle to avoid needle holes. Unfortunately, friction causes crewel yarn to fray if the thread is forced through closely woven twill. To solve this problem I have developed a fabric, Townsend Twill, which is now available in the United States. This twill resembles the wider wale twill which was used in old English embroidery, and it is excellent for crewel embroidery. Woven 54-inches wide, it is the dimension generally preferred by upholsterers.

Square-weave linen is available in many weights but for crewel embroidery a heavy, strong thread is best. Fine square-weave cloth is used for table linens and altar cloths. Coarsely woven square-weave linen which resembles old hand-woven linen is especially attractive for draperies and bedspreads and is available in 92-inch width. For pillows, pictures, and most household decorative items, I recommend square-weave linen with approximately 24 threads-per-inch. This is excellent for crewel embroidery and all creative stitchery. The even weave permits counted thread work and border designs which can be worked on a thread line guide.

EMBROIDERY THREADS

The embroidery design usually determines the type of fabric to be used and the fabric, in turn, determines the thread. One must use his best judgment here for just as it would be inappropriate to embroider a delicate and intricate motif on coarse burlap, it would be equally unsuitable to choose heavy yarns when embroidering on very fine linen.

CREWEL YARN

Genuine crewel embroidery should be worked with genuine crewel yarn. I do not consider all wool threads suitable for this type of embroidery. Good crewel embroidery yarn is a strong, two-strand thread and must have long wool fibrils which have been twisted to prevent hairy ends. The finer crewels will permit a lovely and full blending of colors since more stitches can be used closer together within a design area.

The crewel color chart shown on page 55 illustrates the great variety of beautiful hues which are available in this excellent embroidery yarn.

EMBROIDERY TOOLS

Needles. Good embroidery requires good tools as well as good materials. The most essential tool is, of course, the needle. The size of the needle is determined by both the thread and the fabric to be embroidered. You must experiment to determine which size needle is best for your project. Crewel embroidery should be worked with crewel needles which have long, thin, flat eyes which will hold the thread in position and not allow it to shift and slide as this will cause the yarn to fray. If the needle is too fine it does not prepare a hole large enough for the thread which will cause undue wear on the yarn as it must then be forced through the cloth. A needle which is too large will leave holes in the cloth resulting in unevenly spaced stitches. Townsend Twill and square-weave linen with approximately 24 threads-per-inch is best adapted to number 3 crewel needles.

Hoops. I recommend using wooden embroidery hoops which have a screw type, non-slip adjustment. These polished hardwood frames are well-suited for exacting needlework; they grip well and prevent rust and other stains which may occur when using metal hoops.

There are many styles of hoops. Floor models, lap hoops, and the clamp styles to attach to your table are excellent when one remains seated in the same position. They permit the skilled embroiderer to stitch more easily using both hands, pushing the needle in with one hand and pulling it out with the other.

Hand-held hoops are convenient for most purposes since they hold the work taut, are easy to adjust, and it is a simple matter to change the embroidery work area. Available from 4″ to 10″ sizes, these hand hoops will accommodate most embroidery. Needleworkers with short fingers will find the small sizes easiest to handle.

BULLION STITCH

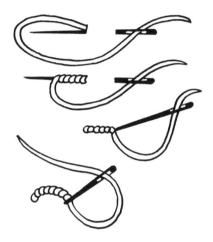

To make a straight, firm *Bullion* stitch: The size of the finished rolled coil is determined by the first stitch established by the needle. The point of the needle must come out at the same spot where the original thread emerged from the fabric. Wind the yarn around the needle until it measures enough to equal the distance of fabric length on the needle. Hold the thread coil and needle firmly between thumb and forefinger of the left hand and pull needle and thread through. Turn the rolled coil back and insert needle again into fabric.

To make a curved Bullion stitch: Follow the same directions but wind more thread on the needle so that it will not lay flat. You can achieve loops of Bullion stitches by making a very small first stitch and winding thread many times around the needle. These loops can then be tacked into position to form rosebuds or flower textures as shown in Plate VIII on page 80.

For best results use a long round needle with a small eye. It will pass more smoothly through the coil which must not be allowed to slip when you are reversing the position of the coil.

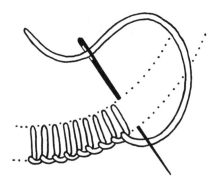

A smooth row of <u>*Buttonhole*</u> stitches needs parallel lines as a guide for the stitches. Begin by bringing the needle out at the bottom line. Stitch into the top line and emerge again at the lower line with the thread under the point of the needle. Do not use an embroidery hoop for this stitch.

There are many variations of Buttonhole stitch. When the stitches are spaced a distance apart, this is called Blanket stitch. When the stitches radiate from the center of a circle they are called Buttonhole Wheels. The Shell stitch consists of a group of Buttonhole stitches slanted to a point. When one Buttonhole stitch slants to the right and the next stitch slants to the left in even rows, this makes a Cross Stitch Buttonhole. Long and Short Buttonhole stitch produces a lovely edge for Long and Short stitches. Many beautiful filling stitches are created by working rows of Buttonhole stitches with the needle entering between stitches in the row above, thus creating a mass effect. Buttonhole stitches are excellent for binding fabric edges.

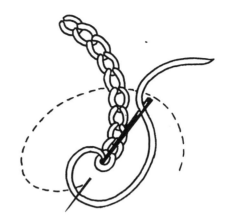

To begin the chain, a loop is formed with the thread while the needle is inserted into the same hole where the thread first emerged from the cloth. Hold the loop down with the thumb of the left hand while sewing a stitch into the fabric. The needle passes over the looped thread. Repeat this in evenly-spaced stitches along a continuous line. Do not pull the thread too tightly. <u>Chain</u> stitches must be worked loosely to keep the chain effect. Several rows of this stitch will produce a beautiful shaded area. However, it is important to begin every row in the same direction. This is essential when using several rows of Chain stitches to form a stem or tree branch.

This stitch is excellent for embroidery on knitted fabric or for sweater decorations because the chained thread allows for stretch if it is worked loosely. The design must, however, consist of scrolls and curves rather than less flexible straight lines which will cause binding on knitted materials.

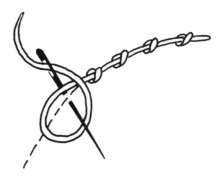

Work from right to left holding the thread down on the line to be embroidered. Insert the needle into the cloth at an angle crossing the line of the pattern. To make small knots keep the needle at a right angle to the line. To make long or chain-effect knots the needle should slant diagonally across the line. The needle passes under the laid thread.

This stitch may be worked with knots spaced close together or wide apart. Entire masses are effectively embroidered in this stitch with the knots spaced closely together creating an effect which resembles French Knots. Rows of _Coral_ stitches were often used in Jacobean embroidery to embellish large leaf areas. Interesting borders may be designed using this stitch in a zigzag fashion or in continuous scroll.

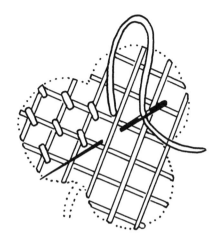

Begin the Trellis stitch by laying evenly-spaced threads in one direction across the space to be filled with all threads parallel to each other. A second layer of stitches is arranged across the first, forming squares resembling a rose trellis fence. These long stitches should appear only on the right side of the embroidery. The reverse side will show short stitches on the outside edge of the design. At the point where the long stitches cross, a small stitch must be sewn to hold the long threads securely in place. This is called a Couching stitch.

This stitch is sometimes called Squared Filling or Tied Cross Stitch. It is very effective for filling large areas. French Knots or Cross Stitches are sometimes used for the Couching stitch. When the squares of fabric between the lines present sufficient space, it is effective to work another complete area of _Couched Trellis_ stitch over the finished design using another color or contrasting shade. The second layer of squares is then placed across the center of the first layer. A hoop must be used for working this stitch.

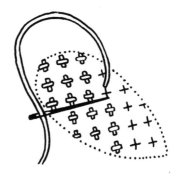

Simple _Cross Stitches_ arranged evenly in a design area are most effective and easy to do. A square-weave linen fabric helps to make
this a simple counted thread pattern but it can also be done in
irregular rows providing the distance between each Cross Stitch is
evenly spaced. For smooth, neat effects it is best to keep the first stitch
in one direction and all cross threads in the other direction.

If you encounter difficulty keeping the Cross Stitches in even rows,
it is sometimes helpful to sew long Trellis stitches in cotton sewing
thread across the area as a guide. These threads can then be clipped
away after the Cross Stitches are sewn.

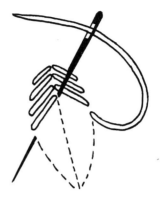

This beautiful stitch is excellent for small leaves since it creates an indented line where the two sides meet. The first stitch begins with the thread emerging from one side. The needle is then inserted at the center line and emerges from the opposite side of the leaf. The point of the needle is again inserted into the center and emerges on the opposite side, one stitch below. Continue working with needle slanting alternately from left to right and right to left forming pairs of stitches which meet in the middle. The back of the embroidery will look exactly like the front since the stitch uses yarn on both sides of the cloth. The _Double Satin_ stitch is easier to sew than two separate sections of Satin stitches because the balanced stitches provide better direction for aiming the needle. This stitch is excellent for heavy lines and large monograms but it is primarily used for leaves as shown in Plate VII on page 77.

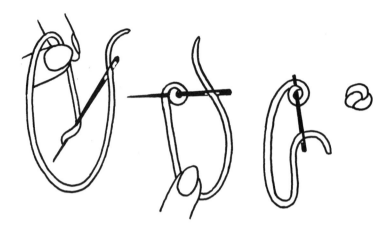

Hold thread taut with thumb and forefinger about two inches from the point where thread emerged from fabric. *Wind the* <u>*needle once*</u> around the thread in a clockwise motion. Lock thread under point of needle with knot formed close to the fabric. Insert point of needle almost in the same place where thread originally emerged from fabric. The result should be a firm bead-like knot with an indented center. Be sure to turn the needle only once around the yarn. This produces a perfect knot. If larger knots are desired use two or three strands of yarn. The use of an embroidery hoop makes this stitch easier to produce in lines and masses.

Embroidered chair seats and items requiring abrasive wear should have firm, tight knots worked in single thread. Loose, bulky knots should be avoided because they will wear off before the remaining smooth stitchery does, leaving unsightly bare spots in the pattern.

<u>French Knots</u> are used for flower centers, lambs' wool effect on animals, filling stitches and for shading large textured areas. The experienced worker can produce beautiful textured lines with rows of neat French Knots. It is possible to work an entire embroidery piece using this stitch alone.

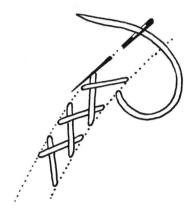

The *Herringbone Stitch* has many variations. It is shown here in its simplest form. On the right side it consists of slanting Cross Stitches. On the reverse side it appears as two rows of Back stitches. Working from left to right, begin with thread emerging on bottom line. Sew a stitch from right to left along top line. The second stitch is sewn from right to left along the bottom line. Continue alternating from top row to bottom row forming slanted Cross Stitches.

This stitch is excellent for stems (see page 76). It works up very quickly and gives a lovely textured line. It can also be used as a filling stitch in small areas. See leaves, in color on page 77.

Closed Herringbone Stitch is worked in the same way with the back stitches touching each other.

Solid Herringbone Stitch is worked with all slanting stitches laid closely together and no fabric is allowed to show between the stitches. Since it creates a padded effect, its use is limited.

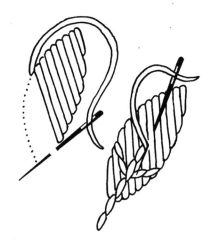

To prepare an area for <u>*Laid Work*</u>, the first step is to sew flat, evenly-spaced stitches across the area to be covered. This is done by taking small stitches along the outside edge, sewing from one side to the opposite side. Keep all stitches side by side with no fabric showing between them. Do not allow thread to twist. Veins of leaves or other design effects are worked over the top of the laid threads using a fine Stem Outline which is made with the needle below the thread and working from left to right to produce a thin, firm line.

For very large areas it is best to begin in the middle and to lay a row of threads with one thread-space between each stitch. Then lay a thread between each thread until the entire area is covered. This diagram illustrates the simplest form of Laid Work. There are many beautiful and elaborate ways of creating effects for Laid Work. Split stitches, Chain or Coral stitches may be substituted for the surface outline. Contrasting threads may be laid across the top and held in place with small Couching or Overcasting stitches. A hoop is essential for doing Laid Work.

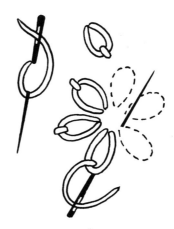

This stitch is also called the Detached Chain stitch. A loop is formed with the thread while the needle is inserted into the same hole where the thread first emerged from the cloth. Hold the loop down with the thumb of the left hand while sewing a stitch into the fabric. The needle passes over the looped thread. The loop is then held in place by a small stitch sewn over the center of the loop.

Lazy Daisy stitches are useful for forming small flowers as shown in the diagram. Larger blossoms with multi-petal effects can be worked with several layers of this stitch embroidered in blending shades. See flower E, on Plate VIII, page 80.

This Detached Chain is often used as a filling stitch to create a speckled effect in a large area. It can also be substituted for a French Knot if it is worked in extremely small stitches.

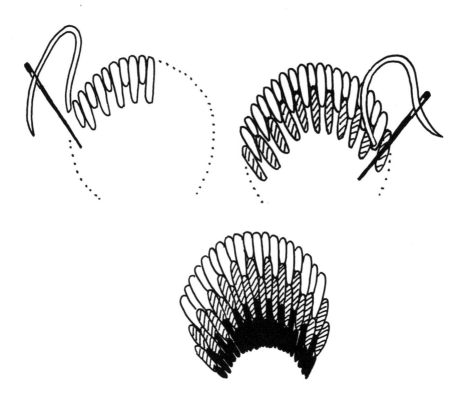

The first row of this stitch is sewn with <u>Long</u> and <u>Short</u> stitches beginning at the center of the outside edge. *Only the outside edge is* worked in these Long and Short stitches. All succeeding rows of stitches are worked in Long stitches.

Begin on the outside edge so that you may aim your stitches into the center of the pattern or into the direction of the area to be embroidered. After the first row of Long and Short stitches is established it will prepare the space for the next row of stitches. The second row of stitches is achieved by stitching up into the tip of the Short stitches and down into the cloth making all stitches the same size as previous Long stitches. Stitching into the tip of the previous row of stitches will split the thread and create a smooth shading of colors. Continue these Long stitches until the area is filled. A few Short stitches are sometimes needed at the end of the space.

All Long and Short stitches should be worked on a hoop. Remember to stitch up into the embroidery and down into the cloth to avoid indentations and needle holes. See Chapter 7 for additional information on Long and Short stitches.

1. Alternating Outline

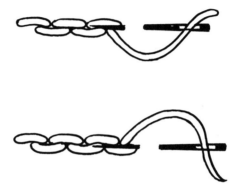

The *Alternating Outline* stitch is worked from left to right. Insert needle into guide line in same manner as for *Crewel* or Stem Outline, however, sew first stitch with thread below the needle and the second stitch with the thread above the needle. Continue along the line in this manner alternating the thread above and below the needle.

This stitch is used for tree trunks and heavy solid lines. It makes what appears to be a double row of Back stitches on the front and a single row of Back stitches on the back of the fabric. Decorative effects can be obtained by inserting contrasting threads through the stitches to form a braid. Outline stitches should not be worked on a hoop and the stitches should not be worked too tightly.

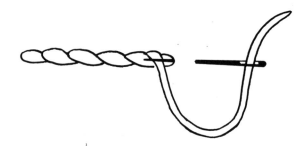

Work from left to right with the thread toward you and the needle stitching into the guide line to be embroidered. Every stitch should touch the previous stitch on the line. The reverse side of your work should look like a perfect row of Back stitches. You will notice that every stitch remains clearly visible. Do not use a hoop.

Try using this stitch in various shades of crewel yarn and arrange several rows together forming a solid area. You will discover that the rows of stitches blend together beautifully. This is why this stitch is called the *Crewel Outline* stitch.

Crewel Outline is not desirable for working fine stems or for embroidering small curved lines. For fine lines use Stem Outline stitch. (See page 61.)

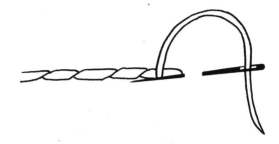

The *Stem Outline* stitch must be worked with the needle inserted into the guide line and with the thread placed above the needle. Sew stitches from left to right with every stitch touching the stitch before it. You will soon discover that the consecutive stitches form a smooth, solid line. These stitches will twist to make what appears to be a continuous stem without separate stitches. This, of course, is why it is called the Stem Outline and it is used for embroidering fine stems and thin delicate outline areas. It is best to take small stitches when turning corners and working around small curved scrolls. Do not use a hoop. The reverse side of this stitch should appear to be a perfect row of Back stitches.

Several rows of the Stem Outline will create firm ridges. If a blending effect is desired use Crewel Outline stitch. (See page 61.)

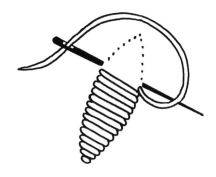

Satin stitch consists of flat stitches laid side by side with the needle entering on one side of the space and emerging on the opposite side. It looks like the easiest stitch to sew but it is very difficult to work perfectly. Avoid using Satin stitch in large areas or with Long stitches because it will not wear well if used in this way. If a large area is to be filled with Satin stitches, it should be divided into several sections. Satin stitches are attractive if they are slanted to create a smooth shading effect.

Beginners may obtain smoother edges if a row of Split stitches is first sewn around the area to be filled with Satin stitches. Victorian embroiderers used thread padding under Satin stitches to create heavy, raised effects. This is not to be recommended for items which are expected to receive wear or constant use since the padded area will wear out before the rest of the embroidery.

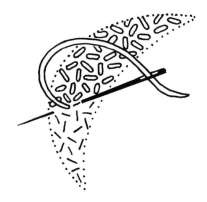

<u>Seed</u> stitches are small Back stitches arranged to fill an open area. They may be worked in Single stitches or in pairs of Back stitches laid closely side by side to create a wider seed effect. Another method is to overlap the second stitch on the understitch with one end slightly apart. The *Seed* stitch is at its best when the stitches are evenly spaced with none of the stitches parallel to the others which surround it. Do not attempt to produce *Seed* stitches with a Running stitch which can easily be pulled out of place when caught by a pointed object. All Seed stitches must be made as Back stitches to secure them as well as to form a rounded thread above the cloth.

The use of Seed stitches is called <u>seeding</u> or <u>speckling</u>. It is effective to use several shades of color when seeding a large area. These colors may be strengthened by working the stitches closely together and lightened by working them farther apart.

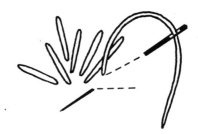

The name of this stitch describes it without need for any further directions. It consists of nothing more than one single line of thread on the fabric. The direction of each stitch must, however, have a purpose. The use of this stitch may be seen in the cornflower blossom G, shown on Plate VIII, page 80.

Single stitches are the delight of beginners and a useful practice for control of the needle when teaching children. However, it has recently come into greater use in free-style creative stitchery where the stitch is symbolic rather than related or conforming to other rhythms or patterns and is worked much like a graphic line.

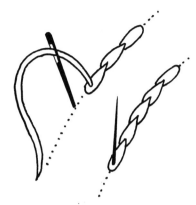

A row of *Split* stitches makes a very fine outline. This must be worked on a hoop to obtain smooth, evenly-spaced stitches. The needle should be inserted up into the previous stitch carefully splitting the middle of the thread. The second action of the needle is to stitch downward to complete the stitch. Rows of this stitch will make beautiful filled areas and can create lovely shaded effects. Many beautiful medieval embroideries were worked entirely in this stitch using silk threads to produce the details in portraits for ecclesiastical embroidery.

This stitch is frequently used in crewel embroidery as an outline edge of a leaf or flower petal before working Long and Short stitches over it. This develops a raised effect to lift the petal or leaf forward from the adjacent area. It is also very helpful to use Split stitch around a pattern which is to be covered with Satin stitches.

The first step of this stitch begins with a small stitch from right to left leaving the thread end above the cloth. This is followed by another stitch to the right of the first and stitching into the first. Before beginning the repeat of these two stitches, a loop should be allowed to form. Continue working along a line with a loop between each pair of stitches. To create shaded effects and for all *Tufted* stitches, it is best to work in even lines. Fine thread requires many small stitches which will have masses of loops on the right side of the embroidery and tiny, flat stitches on the reverse side. When embroidery is completed, clip the top surface to open the loops.

This stitch is also called Carpet stitch because it is used in rug making, and sometimes called Turkey Work since it resembles Turkish carpets. When masses of this Tufted stitch are clipped very short, they can produce an effect of velvet. If the threads are left longer they will create a soft, fluffy area. This stitch is often used to make animals and soft, fuzzy flower centers. The tails of the squirrels on pages 57 and 58 were worked in this stitch.